WYATT EARP IN DALLAS: 1963

WYATT EARP IN DALLAS: 1963

STEVE McCABE

SERAPHIM EDITIONS

Published in 1995 by
Seraphim Editions
1000 Gerrard Street East
P.O. Box 98174
Toronto, Ontario
M4M 3L9

Canadian Cataloguing in Publication Data

McCabe, Steve, 1949-
Wyatt Earp In Dallas: 1963

Poems.
ISBN 0-9699639-0-4

1. Earp, Wyatt 1848-1929 - Poetry.
2. Kennedy, John F. (John Fitzgerald), 1917-1963 - Assassination -
Poetry. I. Title.
PS8575.C32W9 1995   C811'.54   C95-931589-6
PR9199.3.M33W9 1995

Page Layout & Design by Mark Critoph

PRINTED AND BOUND IN CANADA

Special thanks to Tanya Nanavati whose editorial guidance
made this book possible.
Thanks also to Maureen Whyte for her vision of publishing.

for Felicia & Anne

PART 1
JAILHOUSE PROPHECY

☆ WYATT EARP IN DALLAS:1963 ☆
[Part 1: Jailhouse Prophecy]

Wyatt the man
singing, his cell door slamming,
these jailhouse keys are not gonna rust
song;
looks on his sleeping trance prisoner
perplexed beyond belief.
Beyond the edges of town.
Beyond the black sky studded
with misfired diamonds.

He listens the way he listened
as a little polka dot;
the prisoner's breath a harmonica's farewell.
Its last note, before a clean hoof
steps into the shit
of civilization.

Wyatt bends over the whispering prisoner,
listens with the dawn of time
rhinoceros lids;
slides into the swamps of Eden,
around the corner
from Lady Luck's all night saloon.

Wyatt gives the prisoner the dignity of his name.
"Noah Jenkins, you have a visitor."
She smells of apples.
"The widow's daughter
has brought you a pie."

She – a dove with Da Vinci wings
steel lace/sepia sketched/lifting off the page
her face a fresco
stronger than my handcuffs.

Wyatt's shirt is stiff with sweat.
His brothers Virgil and Morgan/vultures hovering
on a mercy mission.
"Prop him up, boys."

"Miss Dove, let me
escort you out."

"Jenkins, I've got to taste the pie."
No weapon in this mouthful.
Only the county fair, when Momma
won the baking contest.

The prisoner tells Wyatt
a crystal river is waiting.
"Where is this stream?
Does it run through my town?
You're smiling, Jenkins.
I won't allow insolence."
It's time for you to face the music
of no music,
to face the face of no eyes.

Wyatt the man, pacing a courtroom,
long black coat
illuminated by a single star.
Wyatt, the night sky fallen
out of orbit – recounting deeds
to a bony wax day-of-the-dead head
nodding/one sad almost melting jowl
kept tight by meanness
propped up by a weak fist.
Wyatt relates earnestly –
"Before you pass sentence . . . "

A banker shot dead in the dead of night:
signing papers/his final foreclosure.
The accused waiting in the parlor,
A disagreement – one shot fired –
prisoner Jenkins found with eyes closed.
"It's not black and white your honor."

"I'll be the judge of that," says the judge
pulling one strand, the wick, from the top of his head.
One day I'll be governer
Across the ocean I'd wear a royal wig.
Pray Lord do tell us
what is black and white.

Wyatt gestured. "This prisoner
whispering in a dream
told me of the banker's nefarious plan."

"As your honor knows . . .
true religion is relieving the affliction of a widow."
James 1:27.

Who put the bee in Wyatt's bonnet?
The judge a dripless candle, is
unmoved by the widow's struggle.
Wyatt's thoughts were framed in disappearing rope.

Wyatt inspired, whirls: a comets tail!
"The bare hands of this so called
pillar of our community strangling her home.
Anointing himself a riverboat captain,
building a paddle-wheel steamer
where she tied her rowboat.
He must have been mad."

"I'll judge madness!" snapped the judge.
Wyatt defers. "Of course,
my job is to bring them to justice.
I don't know why
people dream what they dream."

Prisoner Jenkins stirs. Wyatt hears a whisper;
" . . . Wyatt Earth, Quiet Earp
Quiet Earth, Wyatt Birth . . . "

The judge biting his judicial nails.
"What did he say?"

"A rhyme your honor –
I have here the banker's papers.
Fraudulent allegations of missed payments,
trespassing . . . "
"Enough! Mr. Earp!"
Straightening the wick on his steaming skull,
the root of which descends
into the back of his eyes,
sucking moisture.
His bone and wax de-wigged head
now pronounces sentence on the prisoner:

"Marshall Earp,
who could not be moved?"
Justice brought to the mouth
of a cave.
"I thank you Mr. Earp."
Men like you mopping up the jails –
men who use a shiny tin plate as your shaving mirror
then give it a good wipe
the way I wipe this land.
"Judges salute celestial figures like yourself."
Spinning your desk madly at midnight –
blasting off/rising above the city.
Wyatt I like you right where you are.
Every man has to outgrow the noose.
Back east I was a commissioner of police.
Now I'm a judge. I tuck the truth in at night
and sing it lullabies
to outgrow my hanging branch.
And for that I get this god forsaken circuit
of endless rattlesnake hours.

Have you become a threat to the order of things?
Do you accept the banker's death?
Are we to adhere to this widow's grief?

You are no visionary Mr. Earp.
One tarnished star separates you from the mob.
My burned out eyes glow at the prospect of sharing
the taming of the west with you.

"You want mercy for the prisoner?"
My mercy is a neck broken quickly!
Marshall Earp, when I am governer
my smile will be a whip on the back
of a populace good only for creating wealth.

Of course the banker was justified.
But you don't understand me.

Very well – let's cartwheel
a dance of mercy
with you as the acrobat ring master.

"Mr. Earp,
Keep him alive. Feed him."
Listen to his mutterings on your own time.
In your own home.
"Report to me on my next visit."

Wyatt turns to look Miss Dove in the eye.
He accepts the terms: keeping his ear to
the ground.

Miss Dove fluffs a pillow.
Jenkins wrapped in fresh scrubbed laundry
sinks into his lonely voyage.

"Wake up Wyatt.
The crystal river calls you."

"Jenkins – perhaps you hear a turtle diving."

"No Wyatt. These silver fish are for you."
Words leap from the prisoner's mouth:

☆ WYATT EARP IN DALLAS: 1963 ☆
[PART 1: JAILHOUSE PROPHECY]

"In twilight on the compound
a slippery eel is bagged.
He wears a concrete halo
under a burning flag.

The makers of his sentence
swallow powder burning hot
they pay the good judge Warrant
to say what is is not.

The eel is wriggling backwards
to the alley's hanging tree.
Away from horseless carriages
and a prince named Kenth of Dree.

Shots ring out – the Clanton gang
with friends who wear the star
have rained down poison bullets
on to his rolling car.

Powder explodes, Kenth of Dree
is struck both front and side
disciples of the blister
scatter bent with pride –

A marshall named Quiet Earth
reappears from the grave
spectral, though he knows the law.
The prince should have been saved.

We adhere to a widow's grief
inside the mother cord box.
The eel is bald – no one to help
bit by a ruby fox.

Kenth of Dree mortally shot
by men who hate this earth.
His being swallowed up.
Hell has given birth.

Marshall Earth haunts the grass
where dirty deals were done.
Collecting scraps of evidence
while elsewhere lies are spun."

Wyatt listened: sharp soft/dream shot words –
spectral earth from beyond the grave.
Jenkins floats in a blurry halo.
Cacti under water.

Walking to the jail, remembers/rhymes;
Wyatt Earp, Quiet Earth.
"Why do I think of such things?
Has the prisoner traded places?"

Pausing at a trough
Wyatt sees
a horse dip his hot head
whipped into a lather.
How does a crystal stream speak?

Virgil and Morgan
peas in a pod,
toothpick stuck between the same teeth.

"Boys give me some of that brew."
Tin cup hot as a handle on hell.
A cat's eye gleams in his coffee.

☆ WYATT EARP IN DALLAS:1963 ☆
[PART 1: JAILHOUSE PROPHECY]

Wyatt walks past the O.K. Corral: turns fast –
Thought he heard a heartbeat.
Feels a Clanton/peering from beneath
the bleached conical skull of a bird.

Say isn't that the judge
dining with the Clanton Gang?
I didn't know they had a history.

The Clantons/gunning for Kenth of Dree
arriving in his princely carriage.
What far away hand pays them?
Thin shadowy faces around a camp fire:
Plotting/cups dry.
Wyatt prefers his full.

☆ WYATT EARP IN DALLAS:1963 ☆
[PART 1: JAILHOUSE PROPHECY]

Jenkins is swimming in the river
not crystal like broken glass:
Crystal like the last drop before extinction/
First drop before pleasure.
The river Noah rode like a bucking bronco,
a liquid mare seeping into the earth.

Wyatt walks in the dew.
Jenkins I am dipping my cup into the flood.
The door of sleep: Here come the Clantons –
Scavenger fish lifted by their whiskers.

"Ribbons of dew swirl about Kenth of Dree.
Child of the mystic isles.
Fire consumes his carriage
shattered in the streets of Tombstone.
Red flames spreading:
Dree is floating. Oh dread/dread:
Dree is dead."

"Jenkins wake up!"

"Dree the gardener.
Cattle barons want none of his flowers –
They smell minerals."

The Clantons hack at the sky with curses
its flaming testicle unreachable.
We can shoot out chandeliers –
but that damn THING!
a boiling red eye –
warming his water
bowls scratched with mysterious words
poured over his back by dark haired maidens fair/
while we/no strangers to this land
one with the scorpions and rattlesnakes/
sit parched
slitting open the belly of a mule
for one drop of moisture.

"Wyatt the crystal river swallows me.
A veined mirror,
the blood in an eye decorates your vest.
Your star has become ice."

Kenth of Dree plants Wyatt. Waters him.
No flower of Kenth of Dree
is used for a hanging branch.

Above the garden a ghost ship watches,
the Clantons smell wet wood.

☆ WYATT EARP IN DALLAS:1963 ☆
[PART 1: JAILHOUSE PROPHECY]

And Wyatt, the river carries
this blood/lightning:
"Prince of Dree will float face down
past towns where:
A profane rodent is chewing at the soul
of those who pretend to love the flag.
Whose long fingers fill the earth with poison.
You won't find them Wyatt. They are far away
faces in a box with a cord like I had
attached to my sacred mother."

Wyatt's eyes are hard:
"Who has the cords that are a profanity
to our mother's love?
Is the prince floating outside the widow's house?
Where is the poison?
Virgil, Morgan and I can search all night."

Wyatt twitches to a knock on wood.
"Miss Dove good evening.
Step inside."

"Mr. Earp, as you adhere
to the judge's conditions,
let me help you care for the prisoner."
Her eyes probe the face
flowing from an underwater tomb to Tombstone.

He saved her mother's farm.
Is there more to this
than thanking her lucky star?
The star inside Wyatt's chest leads him through the world:
Pulsating. Metallic medieval.

Miss Dove is pierced by sleep.
A twirling spinning top she digs a groove
in the land between
Wyatt and Jenkins.
Beneath them underground
the wing of an owl slices
a castle tower.

Kenth of Dree
arrives on a subterranean wing;
feather tips interlocking with Miss Dove
inhaling motion.

Jenkins hears the owl.

Her white wing slices Wyatt.

☆ WYATT EARP IN DALLAS:1963 ☆
[PART 1: JAILHOUSE PROPHECY]

Miss Dove longs to cradle magic sleep in her arms
to rock it with the rhythm of America –

She combs his hair.
Washes the stems on his neck:
strokes the flat pulpy leaves too long beneath water.
Her fingertips whisper pressing green pulp to the anvil.
Spreads his hair across the pillow –
a fetal mask rising from the jungle
damp soil clinging to him.
Miss Dove wipes his mouth.

Wyatt Earp – Quiet Earth
escorts Miss Dove to the door.
"You have done enough today."

Jenkins lids suffused/surrendered.
Wyatt turns down the lamp.

Red cape flowing
Dree rises – sinks/
stallion hoofs pound
gold sword jangling
Dree rides to the sea.
Jenkins shoots the banker – Dree's horse
led up a plank
is greeted by a scribe.
"Together we shall discover the wide open space."
Green ship/red sails/Jenkins' eyes close:
Miss Dove puts a finger to his lips:
Shhh . . .

Wyatt's breath falls into pastures
blowing like tumbleweed across the room
to Jenkins the horizon.

Wyatt – tired of whiskey behind the ears
poured over the knees
looks at his hand/turns it over:
A bare wall in moonlight feeling its lonely heartbeat.

When Wyatt was a boy the world was fresh
hanging on a clothes' line.
Twilight rained gooseberries,
Momma served cornbread wrapped in a steaming towel.
Boys in straw hats squinted,
Frogs leapt/cane poles dipped into clear water
catching fish shiny as a baby's ear.

People moved through their town life
the way a salt shaker passes
around the table.

Our childhood friend Lucy
turned her dirt filled pockets inside out.
We all laughed.
Three ant kings and one ant queen:
playing patty cake with a volcano –
home sweet home – Lucy laughed the most.

Tornadoes rip through Missouri.
Wyatt closes his fist on moonlight,
yawns
swims in the water with Jenkins.

Inside the ant hill
Jenkins hands are bleeding
Lucy holds them in her own.
"Noah – you need strong hands to build the ark
let me wash them."

"Wyatt wake up. You were talking in your sleep,"
said Noah.
"Wyatt, I am an ear on the mountain.
Roosters wake to lengths of lumber being cut.
Pounding echoes across the valley.
My hands coil rope/measuring
I decipher the blueprint
received the night before.

As my great ark takes shape
caravans arrive to trade species 2 x 2
we feed them – build stables.
Refugees carry empty jugs – we irrigate. How ironic!
Bagging seeds: storing provisions.

Corrupt judges devour minerals
which nourished ancient roots/they send outlaw gangs
to mock us.
We smear black tar to fill bullet holes.

Walking barefoot over sawdust planks
her midnight gaze is alerted.
White stars withdraw behind a tin sky.
Cradling a sick beast she whirls:
inspired,
capturing the final star."

☆ WYATT EARP IN DALLAS: 1963 ☆
[PART 1: JAILHOUSE PROPHECY]

"Wyatt take your eyes from Miss Dove,"
said Noah.

"Our doors close as the first drops fall.
Flowers float (plant me)
on the surface near the ark (plant me)
bobbing pointlessly against rough shaved
bankers' lips.

Piranhas bite mouthfuls from Kenth of Dree.
Grinning they circle his scribe,
quill pen trembling on calf skin, eyelid thin.

Like the word hunger
my story has been shortened for children."

Wyatt's star faces the future.
His boots crack
beneath a sky
heavy as bone.
He grows red wings to stir the flood.
Whipping wine to sting the judge's head
that sweats profusely.

"Marshall Earp I sense your mood has changed.
Has caring for the prisoner presented any difficulty?"

Wyatt contemplates a tangle of threads
Unraveled by Noah.

The puzzled judge
watches his blue veins pulse
beneath a nicotine stained cuff.
Inwardly he groans.

"What clot of a pronouncement
is Earp about to make?"

"I've been listening," states Wyatt.
Rooted.
His branches shaking in the judge's face.

It can't last forever. This ignoring Earp.

"Your honor, we appreciate the compassion
you have shown,
representing the law
that thousands of years ago
took Noah's boat
across sacred rivers,
poisoned by the people
who hide inside
a mother cord box . . . "

"Marshall Earp! What in God's name are you saying?"

Wyatt's wings red hot
from a pot bellied stove
now press into the judge's
wax temples.

"My god I am melting."
He clutches his head.

Wyatt retreats.

☆ WYATT EARP IN DALLAS:1963 ☆
[PART 1: JAILHOUSE PROPHECY]

The judge leafs through brittle papers:
sucked dry by roots and tentacles
snaking across the desert
to strangle his courtroom decorum.

I'll chop them down and suck their pulp.
This is the law of the roaring flood!

Miss Dove in the back row
feels a breeze through the window.

The judge is smitten.

He telegraphs a purr to her exposed throat:
a silky stem caressed by the red polka dots
of her lady kerchief.
Wouldn't she look nice in the statehouse?
A pretty little charm to drip on his arm.

The judge squints:
"I must examine the banker's loopholes."
That damn prisoner is only firing blanks now.

She studies a cloud.

He watches me.
Thinks I will dance to his rotgut cologne:
sweep his floor littered with bones,
entertain the other wives,
receive his treasures at night/a rusted
skeleton key.

I'll abandon him to his co-conspirators
beneath the shadow of the great Ark.

Noah calls me.
A midnight star clutched to my breast.
I'll walk the heaving planks
caring for the beasts of memory.

Rising, her eyes fire buckshot:
"I volunteer to care for the prisoner."

Swirls of confusion stain the judge's face.

Wyatt had read the eyes
unbuttoning her frontier clothing –
he makes his move.

"Your honor I have benefitted
from the exchange of whispers:
at times the prisoner describes places and faces
that may relate to threats
made against the Prince,
Kenth of Dree.
It is of vital importance
that this prisoner
remain in my care.
Miss Dove may assist me
in my house."

The judge was trapped.
His challenge two fold.
Keeping Miss Dove and Wyatt Earp
from late hours together
(Who's going to wash him tonight?)
And restricting Earp's access
to dream information
Noah Jenkins has somehow obtained.
(I may be implicated.)

☆ WYATT EARP IN DALLAS:1963 ☆
[PART 1: JAILHOUSE PROPHECY]

"Miss Dove, I assign you
to care for this prisoner
in the schoolhouse."

Reaching for the court document
she touched his fingers.
The silhouette of her throat
stood against
the mouth of his solitary cave.

Birds of prey
chained to the pulse on his wrist
beat him with their wings.

Words of terror form in his throat:
"Miss Dove will you join me for dinner?"

Now Wyatt is free to turn this place upside down.

Wyatt, Virgil and Morgan
carry the prisoner through shadowed streets.

Doc Holiday joins them.
His feverish cough
barking into the cool night air
ruled by a crescent moon.

"Good of you to help, Doc."

"Wyatt, the Clantons are bragging;
Earp won't interfere
he's too busy listening
to dreams."

Wyatt tapped his silver star:
"The Clanton gang is a festering sore."

☆ W Y A T T   E A R P   I N   D A L L A S : 1 9 6 3 ☆
[PART 1: JAILHOUSE PROPHECY]

He lifts water to Noah's lips,
the soothsayer asleep as usual
in his chamber of dreams.

If you dream your way out of this sleep,
escape!
Fly with her on white wings!

The prisoner turns his moist lips
from the cup.
One arm falls,
a finger points.
"We are in their midst," he said
and never spoke another word
to Wyatt, crouching with a kerosene lamp,
peering between the floorboards.

Shimmering like smoke
in the opposite corner
his childhood friend Lucy appears;
"I saw you watching the ants.
Millions of them
were on the ark's great voyage,
building temples of hardened sand.
It's what they do
when a deluge approaches."

Wyatt remembered
a tornado and the flood
that swept Lucy away.
He is startled
that she is so small
telling him
how she has traveled
from the other side
where dreams are seeds
in the quiet earth
and the law a storm
above the rain, falling to reveal
the quiet birth
of Marshall Earth.

She faded
whispering a promise;
"The crystal river shines like dew.
Kenth of Dree travels to you."

Sunrise found Wyatt Earp watching Miss Dove's window.

At noon Virgil and Morgan lift his boots
off the desk
he wakes groggy
talking in a trance;
"These jailhouse keys are not gonna rust."

"Wyatt;
The horses kicking up dust
on the outskirts of town
are heading
for the O.K. Corral,
where the Clanton gang
waits in hiding
for Kenth of Dree."

PART 2
NOVEMBER

In the heart of Noah's Ark
(straw heat womb)
is violence we tried to flee.
The killing of Kennedy
is death replayed on a mother cord box.

Auras of this sacrifice
surround a cola machine.
Lee Oswald fumbles for change
in the book depository lunchroom/
presses his selection
as a widow cries out.

Noah steered hard in the rain
avoiding a city skyline.

Germs on the floor
multiplied like raw amoebas.
Yesterday's extinction
is today's head cold.

It was dry in Dallas at noon.
Jackie felt rain on her shoulder.

On the rooftop stood a man,
red stains brilliant on his vest.
He studied Oswald as the dove circled him.

Noah had released her for flight
to return with fresh greenery
proving that Camelot did exist.

She glided to the glint
of Wyatt Earp's star.

Oswald renounced the flood
as the first shots rained down.
He swallowed a wishbone
knowing enough
to prepare for his bed
in the earth.

☆ WYATT EARP IN DALLAS: 1963 ☆
[PART 2: NOVEMBER]

Noah's kitchen was getting low.
Wyatt threw a bag on board.
Vegetarian hyenas sniffed it.
It only contained words
to create a curtain of rain.   .

Noah read the Warren Report.
Trapped in thunder,
dark and heaving as the ribs
of an exhausted god,
he knew terror.

This document
was a handful of seeds
thrown in the face
of an advancing scribe.

Open umbrellas create an illusion
of isolation
from the death of the dove.

Wyatt Earp traveled
in the manner of spirit life
(olive trees dreaming)
to the center of ominous dread.

"Welcome to Dallas, Mr. President."

Wyatt smelled ambush
thick as crocodiles.
He measured trajectories
blinking at
the slow motion motorcade,
eggs in the nest
presented to the holy hammer
of destruction.
State sanctioned clerics
invoke blessings
disguised as perfectly sane butterflies.

"Look, there's Jackie!"
Smiling
in a black and white photograph.

Explosions filled the air.
"What was that?"

Blood shadows
snake along the ground
rising as horror trees.
Running men pass off guns
with jet fighter teeth clenched,
black and white sunglasses
smashed underfoot.

Wyatt not buffaloed,
selflessly tried to warn Jack.

Twisting dials on a jammed radio
Wyatt took a slug through the heart.
How many Clantons were there?

Kennedy's spirit sped howling
as Wyatt sank to the roadside.
The shadow of Noah
intersecting with the plot
passed over his boots.
The Ark sliced into secret code
crackling static.

The slain politician
buried his head in dry straw.

Noah's eye was compassionate.
"Please sign our guest book Mr. President."
Only one name was above his:
Marshall Quiet Earth.

Torn and tragic,
a twilight's last gleaming,
Jack seemed confused by the smell
of feathers and fur.

Noah served him a cup of brew.
He spit it out.
"My body is not fit to drink."

Wyatt Earp covered his tracks
backing towards the Ark.

"Mr. President you are soaking wet,"
said Wyatt.

Jack had passed through a great flood
hurtling past the blind
in brightly lit dark.
They lay in decorated graves
wearing crowns
cheering him.
Jack thought first of their vote
realizing with a jolt
"This is where I am."

Wyatt felt penetrating eyes outside the ark
sending chills up his spine.

He said, "Mr. President,
Noah and I are old friends,
it started with a crime
involving a widow.
The story goes deeper than ore.
Someday I'll tell you."

☆ WYATT EARP IN DALLAS:1963 ☆
[PART 2: NOVEMBER]

Noah placed a stone
in Jack's lap.
He cradled it with closed eyes.
First dreaming of the motorcade
then traveling backwards
to a jail and warm lemonade.

He smelled sacrifice.
Its magnetic eyes
fixed
on a heat soaked O.K. Corral.

Kenth of Dree falling
raised a cloud of dust.
The memory of this was in the stone
and in the wind
inside the stone.

Dree survived to plant flowers
fragrant even in November.

Thousands raised their hands
to moan
while a widow chewed her hair.

The sky was torn and cloudy
grey ice fell like lead
exploding the eggs.

Was it a lone gunman?
The military-industrial salute
one magic bullet?

Noah covered in dust
nudged his boat to land.

A sound like thunder woke the animals.
From inside a low flying plane
the widow waved her gloved hand.
Wyatt Earp removed his hat.
"Belief in true law stirs me.
Are we dealing with pomp and circumstance
(dignitary plotters at the funeral)
to decoy us
into abandoning the twin dead boys?"

Richard Nixon approached in a truck
belching exhaust
igniting straw on Noah's deck.

☆ WYATT EARP IN DALLAS: 1963 ☆
[PART 2: NOVEMBER]

Wyatt Earp
never too proud to ask for help
held the sun in place
casting Dallas into darkness.

The deer and the antelope stare at a boat
their cousins sailed in long ago
hearing shots that were not fired.

A rainbow at Wyatt's feet
is reflected in the water pail.
Kennedy sits as if behind his desk,
"You created havoc with their conspiracy."

The desert dove
ripped cactus
to feed Wyatt Earp
who dreams a president
never died,
and drinks coffee
made from Noah's rain.

The memory of this
is in the stone
and in the wind
inside the stone.

A voodoo curse on stilts
lined the motorcade route
casting its spell.
Kennedy was dead.

A calculated killer
lit up,
flicking his match skyward.
"Holy god," muttered Noah
dashing to flickering straw.

Generous Noah
provided the use of his vessel
to those on missions of goodwill.
He'd be the first to admit
that living in isolation and damp clothing
was no substitute for good cheer.
Besides
Noah was hungry for news of the world.

☆ WYATT EARP IN DALLAS:1963 ☆
[PART 2: NOVEMBER]

The smell of wet wood
drove him crazy.
The interior of the ark
sweated like grapefruit.
He accepted that his payment for construction
was survival.

Noah was feeling rather foul
passing over Dallas at noon.
The motorcade caught his eye.
He'd seen many parades,
most notably a sarcastic festival
bidding him adieu
as the rains began.

Simultaneous
puffs of smoke
erupting beneath him
alerted him to danger.
He'd put out one fire already.

The widow wearing brain
crawled to flickering matter.
As if a miracle
the car picked up speed
after the final volley.

Wyatt Earp appeared from deep space
holding a smoldering flag.

Noah opened a hatch
and dumped out a bale of straw.
It fell like hair,
breaking apart over Dallas.
Sirens wailed/
a thousand faces felt smooth as sand
to the blind widow.
Her fingers searched for his head.
Straw covered her
falling into the limousine
speeding for the hospital.

☆ WYATT EARP IN DALLAS: 1963 ☆
[PART 2: NOVEMBER]

As a lawman
Wyatt knew
not to follow the straw.
You look for the guy with the gun.
You follow him to his cheap hotel.
You watch him pack his bag.
You see him climb into the stage
paying with thirty silver pieces
wrapped in a burning flag.

Wyatt twisted dials on a jammed radio.

"Deputize me dammit," muttered Noah.
He paced starboard.
Let this sea fall to the ground
lashing the lips
of those drowned
at police headquarters.
"For forty days I have been here
each day a thousand years.
I exist only in the memory of my race."
Noah dropped an anchor.

Lee tried to escape
gasping for breath
climbing the knots in his head
a walking palm print
for extinct eyes to read.

Below him
confusion and clarity swirled
thick as fish eggs
captured in buckets and strained
by the Warren Commission
for the Marie Antoinette
of national law enforcement,
J. Edgar Hoover.
Sitting in his electric chair
arranging for Lee's palm print
to stain Old Glory,
further evidence
in a black and white photograph.

Hoover conjured images of Betsy Ross
working on the flag.
She would have fallen for Kennedy,
allowing young Jack to sew on a star.

Reptilian in his rage
he scratched the face of his attendant
handling mail order rifle catalogues.

President Kennedy pale-faced
knocked on Noah's door.
Rushing animals
freaked by gunfire
brushed him back.
He stared at species no longer here
linking their disappearance
to the Lone Star State
previously visited by his advance security team.

Lee panting
scaled the rope
in a personal flood
swept away by his own blood.

A nation harnessed in the cave
sent Lee scrambling.
"You are to defect,
providing Moscow with classified
U2 data."
Lee smirked. He bloomed.

His birthday party had a guest list
of one.
The candles on his cake
were priestly snakes
warming him with reassurance.

He stood
in the shadows
connecting dots.
(The secret sex of political intrigue.)

His fingertips
sucked in dangerous weather.
Voltage crept below ground
rising as horror trees.

Lee stood at the cola machine
in the book depository lunchroom
telling T.V. cameras,
"I can prove I was a patsy.
I learned to tolerate noise
on their old sewing machines."
He reached in his pocket
producing needles as proof.
"Counter insurgency experts
removed the stars I stitched.
Now they fly on our nations flag."

Nixon was forced to stop his truck.
Protesters demanding clean water
thrust their star-shaped scars
in his face.

Next to him sat a cleric
disguised as a perfectly sane butterfly
cautioning the mob of divine anger.

If Lee released his grip how far through time
. would he fall?
With no controller egging him on
he could only impersonate
his adrift self.

Distant choirs chanted
as Lee attached himself to the ark,
sucking its ribs
like an eel.

This universe is Wyatt's to patrol.
He wraps anarchy
in the cocoon of true law.
"Let that boy cool his heels.
He'll behave."
Lee responded in perfect Russian.
"Thank you."

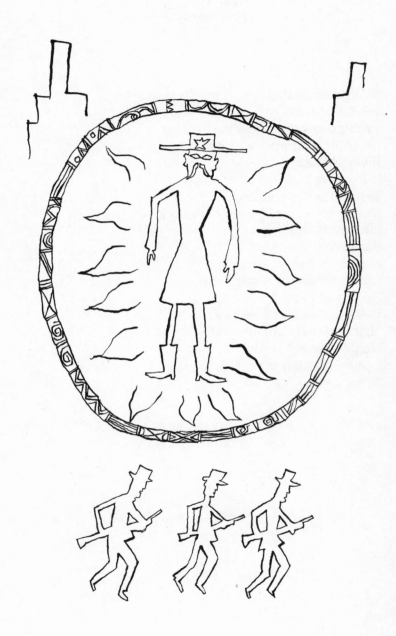

"Welcome to Dallas Mr. President."
Perched on stilts
marksmen deliver their fatal blow.

Noah calmed the shaken president.
"Never forget that you were charmed
by the world spinning."

Jack admitted to his suspicions.
"I was told the shadowy figures
were bankers arriving
to play the flute."

The trees in Dallas prepared for winter.
Shame walked autumn hand in hand.
Noah's anchor landed
cutting through the grass.

Lee Harvey held the boat
sucking barnacles
like it was momma.

"Isn't it my right as an American citizen
to be let in?"
But deep within himself he knew
that he was a bit player
in the history of myth.

Noah unlocked a wooden box
and placed a rounded stone
in Jack's lap.

Binocular agents
lined the motorcade route
viewing from vacant office vantage points
witnesses without eyes.

Sick in its health
the seeing eye plague
dictated this statement:
"School book depository
sixth floor
proved and prayed over
by an all seeing eye."

Earp circumventing
the seeing eye plague
experienced
the birth of Quiet Earth.

Earp born into
the dream of seeds
fallen into earth,
now into Earp
flowering.

Wyatt stares
into the hypnotic pupil of the plague;
the outlines of an interlocking maze
become visible.
Suddenly thrusting forward
a palm covers his eyes.
Its wrist smells of rotgut cologne.
The judge who craved Miss Dove!

The seeing eye plague
turns evidence into innocence,
adolescents into prostitutes
outside the casinos of Havana,
paying their parents
a bag of flour, postponing starvation.
"Cuba was ours!"
A nation refining sugar
for our breakfast.

We wore silk and pinstripes.
Think of us as the boys Betsy Ross bandaged.
Helping us to our desk
within the cavernous seeing eye plague,
bureau of disinformation.

"We see for you."

Dallas, forget the dead witnesses.
Forget Nixon's belching truck.
Forget your true place in history.

Raise your umbrellas.
Do not launch inquiries.
Do not form mobs with torches.

We have a plan for you.
Line the motorcade route with cheerleaders,
tassels and cowgirl hats.

President Kennedy attended the annual
Army – Navy game.
He enjoyed himself.
The plan was ready.

Wyatt's boot hit the deck.
"Well made," he said.
Noah looked at what his bare hands built,
"Cubits are like your western square dance.
Points of measurement
and floor lines to cross."

The president found a fragment
of the infernal
lodged in his skull.
Wyatt handled the evidence.
He gestured at Dallas.
"Texas has always been lawless.
Like a steer tearing down a fence.
The opposite of that
creeping motorcade."

Jack thought of Jackie
scrambling
to retrieve a portion
of his flickering brain
as black hooks from inquisition chambers
clawed at her.

Betsy Ross would have dropped her kettle
in astonishment
at the betrayal in full flight.

The wild teeth of conspirators
rip her flag to shreds.
"You have names of witnesses."
"I have no names."

She only wanted to bandage Kennedy.

Candles with cold black flames
illuminate the maze
within the blinding plague.

"Is this the last of the past?"
inquired J.F.K.

Betsy Ross was inconsolable
concerning the cold flame future
poisoning skies
and the earth,
belching smoke from a truck
sold by a man
with a five o'clock shadow.

Jack didn't know he was hunted.

PART 3
AUTHOR'S NOTE

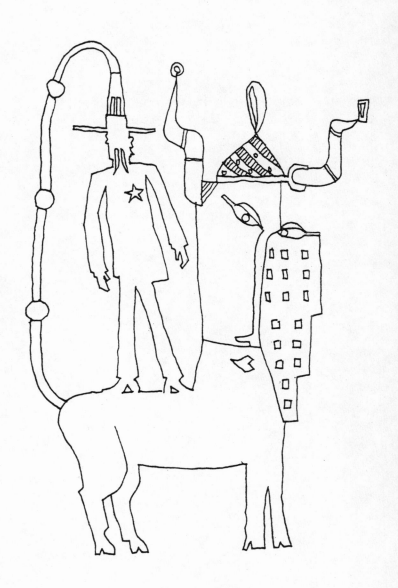

As a boy of thirteen
my parents took me
to see the President
of the United States
in an open air motorcade
festive flag in my hand.

I had been told
that if I studied
and prayed
one day I might be president.

I held the flag while
mother and I stood on the hill.
Father disappeared to buy film.
A shadow
darkened our faces,
tilted skywards
bullets hit the Ark,
splintering wood.
"Look Mother, the President is dead."

Echoes screamed within me.
I dropped my flag.

Terrified, we heard the roars
of animals,
when a small fire
sparked by the exhaust from a truck
poisoned them.
The Ark rose
heavy as judgement.

I looked for my father.
His search had taken him
to distant continents.
My mother wore a black veil
fluttered down from above.

I've returned Novembers since
to where my flag was trampled.
My feet
feel the life of the earth
through my Sunday shoes.

Agents
telephone my home
saying that Betsy Ross
is an illusion,
and that the earth
(adhering to no grief)
is waiting to be sold
to the highest bidder.

Miss Dove washed the eyes of a thirteen year old boy.
The only jungle
that he would fight in
was memory.